LOUIS
SACHAR

ALL ABOUT THE AUTHOR™

LOUIS SACHAR

PHILIP WOLNY AND MEG GREENE

ROSEN
PUBLISHING®

New York

Published in 2016 by The Rosen Publishing Group, Inc.
29 East 21st Street, New York, NY 10010

Copyright © 2016 by The Rosen Publishing Group, Inc.

First Edition

Library of Congress CataloginginPublication Data

Wolny, Philip.
Louis Sachar/Philip Wolny & Meg Greene.—First edition.
    pages cm
Includes bibliographical references and index.
ISBN 978-1-4994-6264-7 (library bound)
1. Sachar, Louis, 1954- —Juvenile literature. 2. Authors, American—20th century—Biography—Juvenile literature. 3. Children's literature—Authorship—Juvenile literature. I. Wolny, Philip. II. Title.
PS3569.A226Z674 2016
813'.54—dc23
[B]
                                                    2015033282

Manufactured in China

CONTENTS

A juvenile detention camp where boys dig holes in the ground around the clock may seem like a grim setting for a young adult novel. Meanwhile, the main character of the book is plagued by bad luck, inherited through the generations from a great-great grandfather. He ends up a prisoner of this camp, where the warden makes boys dig holes around the clock. In anyone else's hands, this premise for a work of fiction could have failed spectacularly. But for celebrated young-adult novelist Louis Sachar (pronounced SACK-er), it proved a winning formula for his best known work, the 1998 novel *Holes*.

Many of Sachar's other books have had equally strange, left-of-center elements: an elementary school thirty stories high; a strangely sympathetic school bully; a secret club known as Pig City; a nine-year-old redhead accused of picking his nose; and so forth. Louis Sachar has used all of these elements in his books for young readers in a career now spanning more than three decades.

Since 1978, Sachar has produced a diverse and popular body of work—twenty-five books to date—that has earned him fans of all ages. Many of his books, such as *Sideways Stories from Wayside School* (1978), *Dogs Don't Tell Jokes* (1991), and *There's a Boy in the Girls' Bathroom* (1987), appear on library and school reading lists throughout the

Louis Sachar has been a favorite young-adult fiction author for more than three decades. His books are often humorous and portray outsiders and misfits.

United States and Canada. Even the most skeptical reader might find him- or herself drawn into Sachar's silly and always offbeat worlds. Louis Sachar's novels are often praised for their humorous but realistic depiction of characters' feelings and relationships, and they are celebrated for cleverly charting the bumpy road to adulthood all young people take.

Sachar cites the influence of his older brother in his eventual blossoming as a writer. He said, "I'd always looked up [to] and tried to emulate [imitate] my older brother. Andy has had more of an influence on my tastes and my outlook than anyone. If he had been the type of person who had gone to business school and went to work for a big-eight accounting firm, I doubt I would be here today."

Sachar has tried to respect the intelligence and sophistication of young readers in his written work, and this approach shines through in his narratives. He also dismisses the idea that writing for kids is tremendously different from writing for older readers. Reading adult literature has informed his young adult books, in fact.

At the same time, there are aspects of childhood that Sachar is able to translate to the page that make his portrayals of young characters ring especially true. His work remains a testament to the fact that writing successfully for young people can be a delicate balancing act that also ties together many different threads. Unusual characters, sensitivity and understanding for his readership, humor, and some serious chops and experience as a writer guarantee that Louis Sachar's works will continue to be popular among young people for many years to come.

ONE

FROM TEACHER TO LAWYER TO WRITER

The young man who would grow up and become the popular author Louis Sacher had a normal, generally happy middle-class childhood from the very beginning. Sachar arrived in the world during the Baby Boom of the postwar era, a time of relative prosperity in the United States. He was born on March 20, 1954, in East Meadow, New York, a suburb of New York City. He was the second son of Robert J. Sachar, a salesman, and Ruth Raybin Sachar, a real estate broker.

When young Louis was nine, his parents, his older brother Andy, and he moved to Tustin, California, a town in Orange County. The landscape of his new home-town during the early 1960s was teeming with orange groves. Sachar remembered them fondly later. His group of friends cut through the orange groves on their way to school and pelted each other with oranges on the way home. He later lamented how many of these orange groves disappeared as suburban and strip-mall development slowly took over the area.

Speaking about his time at Barnum Woods School in East Meadow and then Red Hill School in Tustin, Sachar recalled that "nothing especially traumatic" happened to him. For the most part, he enjoyed school, got good grades, liked math, and played Little League baseball. Sachar also remembers having "a really mean" fifth-grade teacher. "She just seemed to pick on me," he recalled in an interview on his website, Louissacher.com. In the sixth grade, when students misbehaved, the teacher made them copy pages out of the dictionary as a punishment. Sachar never forgot that punishment and would later put it to use in *Sixth Grade Secrets* (1987).

A WRITER BLOOMS

Like many authors, Louis really began to learn how to write by reading. E. B. White, the author of the classic children's book *Charlotte's Web* (1952), was one of Louis's favorite writers and one of his first and most important influences. Even at an

One of Sachar's heroes was E. B. White. White was most famous for his children's literature classic, *Charlotte's Web*. Like Sachar, White was a dog lover, and he is shown here working as his pet dachshund, Minnie, looks on in this 1948 photo.

early age, his favorite writers became his heroes, and he sought to emulate them. Not until high school, though, did Louis begin to enjoy reading on a deeper level. A bit of a teenage rebel, he wore his hair long despite official reprimands and instructions to cut it. Luckily, his parents were understanding and gave him much leeway during his high school years.

Louis first tried his hand at writing in high school. He wrote a story called "Apple Power," which was about a mean teacher named Mrs. Gorf, who turned her students into apples. "I wrote the first Mrs. Gorf story as an assignment in a creative writing class in high school," he noted later. His teacher was unimpressed and thought Louis hadn't taken the assignment seriously. But the young writer always thought it was a good story. Much later, the students at an elementary school where Sachar worked as a teacher's aide while attending college also enjoyed the story. In fact, the positive response from the students, Sachar noted, made him reconsider writing as a pasttime, even a career. He was thus inspired to write longer stories.

In 1972, eighteen-year-old Louis Sachar headed back east to attend Antioch College in Ohio. When his father died during his freshman year, he returned to California to be with his mother. Then Sachar decided to take a semester off before returning to school. To make money, he found a job as a door-to-door salesman. Sachar worked for Fuller Brush (a leading manufacturer of cleaning supplies, brushes, and brooms) for a few months and actually did very well. His employers were convinced he should continue as a salesman rather than go back to school.

The next fall, however, Sachar was back at college, but because he had decided to stay closer to home, he enrolled at the University of California at Berkeley, where he majored in economics. Sachar's interest in becoming a writer had not diminished. Besides his required classes, he signed up for some creative writing courses. He read everything he could, though he disliked many of his English classes

A close-up of a keyboard with Cyrillic characters. Cyrillic alphabets are used in the written languages of many nations, including Russia. Sachar found it harder than he thought to delve into Russian classics in their original language.

because he felt the instructors overanalyzed many of the works.

At one point, Sachar decided to study Russian. He was perhaps a bit overly ambitious since he hoped to read Russian classics in their original language. Despite his good intentions, Sachar soon found that Russian was not for him. A week into the semester, he dropped out of the class.

THE ACCIDENTAL TEACHER

It was by accident that Sachar found the answer to what he should study instead of Russian. One day, a young girl was handing out leaflets on campus seeking teacher's aides for her elementary school. The aides could also earn three units of credit. As a teacher's aide, Sachar could earn the exact number of credits needed to make up for the Russian language course he had dropped. In addition to that, Sachar thought the job sounded easy—there was no homework to do and no classes to take. Not really thinking about what he was getting into (aside from the fact that he thought it would be pretty easy), Sachar signed on. In a way, it was an unexpected path to take. Sachar had little experience with children—he had never really been around them, much less worked with them in a school setting, and he was not particularly interested in them.

Sachar was in for a surprise. His experience at Hillside Elementary School (where he earned his three credits for being a teacher's aide) proved to be much more than an easy way to make up for the dropped Russian course. Working as a teacher's aide soon became one of his favorite college experiences. He also began spending more time with the children, and he was promoted to noontime supervisor, which meant he monitored the playground during recess. For Sachar, supervising often meant playing. Because of this, he earned the title "Louis, the Yard Teacher" from the students.

A SCHOOL TALE

As Sachar was preparing to graduate, he began writing a children's story because, as he told the *Austin Chronicle* in 2002, "I didn't like any of the little stories that they [the students at Hillside Elementary] were reading." Influenced by Damon Runyon's *In Our Town* (1946), a book of interconnected stories, Sachar wrote his own series based on events at a school he created called Wayside.

Like Runyon's offbeat characters, the students of Wayside were also quite unusual. (Some of the Wayside students were given the names of some of the students Sachar had known at Hillside.) Included among the Wayside cast of characters is Mrs. Jewl, whom Sachar based on the real-life teacher Mrs. Jukes, who taught at Hillside Elementary and for whom Sachar had worked as a teacher's aide. Sachar even had a character named Louis the Yard Teacher in his book.

Although times had changed since he was a student in Tustin, having orange fights with his friends on their way home from school, Sachar believed that kids were still basically the same as they were when he was young. Because a lot of the inspiration for Wayside came from his own experiences and feelings, Sachar felt that *Sideways Stories from Wayside School* would strike a chord with elementary and middle school readers.

Sachar graduated from college in 1976 with a degree in economics. After graduation, he moved to Norwalk, Connecticut, where he worked as a shipping manager for Beldoch Industries, a manufacturer of women's sweaters. In the evenings, he wrote. Sachar was fired from his job after seven months and decided to apply to law school. In the fall of 1977, he returned to California to study law

Seen here is the view from the twenty-fourth floor of the University of California's Hastings College of Law residence hall, McAllister Tower. Sachar's attendance at Hastings came at the same time that he was jump-starting his writing career.

at Hastings College of Law of the University of California at San Francisco. In the meantime, Sachar mailed the manuscript of *Sideways Stories from Wayside School* to ten publishers.

A SCHOOL LESS ORDINARY

What began as a regular semester for a first-year law student soon took a surprising turn. During his very first week of law school, a publisher agreed to put out his first book. Thus would begin a years-long struggle by Sachar to decide whether his destiny lay in writing or being a lawyer. If the book had been a failure, his decision might have been easier. However, *Sideways Stories from Wayside School* enjoyed enough success to convince Sachar that it made sense for him to keep writing.

Sideways Stories is about a unique school—the construction workers who built the school had some trouble following directions (and that's putting it mildly), and instead of being thirty classrooms long and one story high, it's one classroom long and thirty stories high. As a result, daily life at Wayside School is anything but ordinary. In the book, each chapter focuses on a particular student or teacher. Many of the students are the pupils of Mrs. Jewl, the school's favorite teacher, whose classroom is on the thirtieth floor.

Each of Sachar's characters possesses

Part of Sachar's inspiration for Wayside School was his father working at the Empire State Building.

an unusual trait. Among them are Joe, who can't count but who somehow always manages to get the right answers, and Todd, who gets into trouble every day although he doesn't do anything wrong. Meanwhile, John can only read while standing on his head. Sammi's favorite item of clothing is a raincoat, but he also smells bad. In one story, a student named Jason is stuck to his seat by a large wad of chewing gum. And though his teacher tries throwing ice water on him to make the gum brittle enough to be broken, Jason remains stuck. The teacher then turns Jason's chair upside down, but that does not work either. The teacher even considers cutting Jason's pants off.

Sachar also included Mrs. Gorf, the teacher from "Apple Power." Still the meanest teacher, Mrs. Gorf turns her students into apples when they do something to displease her, such as misbehave in class or not know the right answer to a question. When asked how he managed to think of all the silly things that happen at Wayside School, Sachar said, according to Louissacher.com, "I sit at my desk and I just try to think. It may be because the life of a writer is somewhat boring, sitting alone in a room, in front of a computer screen. It forces my mind to come up with crazy things."

MAKING A MARK WITH
WAYSIDE SCHOOL

While young readers responded with enthusiasm to the weird goings-on at Wayside School, some adult critics were not as favorably impressed. Some reviewers thought that the book's story line was lacking and that the book had no focus. Others felt that the humor was forced and that the writing was pedestrian, or dull. Ultimately, though, kids loved the book, and many teachers liked it, too. Its short chapters and funny dialogue made the book easy to read aloud in classrooms. Over the years, any mixed reviews or initial doubts about the book faded into memory, and it has become a childhood favorite for many readers.

Even though *Sideways Stories from Wayside School* struck a chord with children and teachers, the book was initially difficult to find, in part because the publisher had not distributed it very effectively. As a result, the book didn't sell many copies, and the idea of Sachar supporting himself as a writer seemed unlikely. He continued his legal studies, as a backup plan for a livelihood.

Even today, after much success with a variety of young adult books, *Sideways Stories* remains special for Sachar. He has expressed that it was the work he had the most fun with throughout the years.

PART-TIME LAWYER, FULL-TIME WRITER

In 1980, at the age of twenty-six, Sachar earned his law degree and prepared to take the bar exam, a test that law students must pass after they graduate in order to practice law. Sachar stayed up all night waiting for the results. He passed, but he was not excited about becoming a lawyer. All he wanted to do was write children's books.

In the end, Sachar compromised. He worked part-time as a lawyer, which allowed him the freedom he needed to write. Sachar usually wrote in the mornings and practiced law in the afternoons. The transition wasn't easy.

One of the toughest aspects was making the switch from being creative in the morning, and, say, putting on a suit and tie for a one o'clock deposition or other legal appointment. Sachar ceased stressing over how to balance his legal and literary careers, opting to go with the flow. For now, he would do both, but he hoped to eventually become just a writer, filling his time with the livelihood he had grown to love.

A WRITER FINDS HIS VOICE

A handful of writers experience overnight success, some of them with their first or second major works. Sachar paid his dues, slowly but surely. He put in time and continued writing, even as his legal career provided a steady meal ticket. His books during the early 1980s explored a variety of themes and character studies. These included children and adolesecents coming of age and learning how to cope with their shortcomings and also how to hone their talents. The protagonists of Sachar's tales tended to range in age from eight to twelve years old.

Sachar's most memorable characters are "empathetic [engaging] misfits," according to an article from *Texas Monthly*. Outcasts among their peers and

Being an outsider, misfit, victim, or other unfortunate outcast is one of the most common themes in Sachar's work. It is one reason many young readers can identify with Sachar's characters and situations.

sometimes their own families, they include bookworms, class clowns, bullies, and klutzes. Despite their shortcomings, these young people possess some endearing qualities. To keep the stories from becoming too moralistic, Sachar injected his silly and offbeat brand of humor, which left some adults scratching their heads but most children howling with laughter.

JOHNNY'S IN THE BASEMENT

In 1981, Sachar published his second book, *Johnny's in the Basement*. The main character, Johnny Laxatayl, spends most of his time in the basement, where his parents won't bother him. In creating Johnny's last name, Sachar drew on his love of puns. "Laxatayl" is a play on the phrase "lacks a tail," and it refers to Johnny's resemblance to a neighborhood dog named Popover.

Johnny's claim to fame is his amazing bottle cap collection. His world has changed since he has turned eleven, and the way Johnny sees it, the changes are not for the better. For his birthday, he receives presents more fitting for an adult, such as socks and underwear. Worst of all, he gets dance lessons. Meanwhile, his parents have decided that it's time for him to grow up and start doing chores like washing the dishes and taking out the trash. Growing up doesn't seem like much fun. However, one day at dancing school, he meets Valerie Plum. She hates dance school even more than Johnny does, and the two become fast friends.

Johnny comes into conflict with his parents over his bottle cap collection. Meeting Valerie serves as a catalyst for his subsequent actions. The story depicts humorously the lengths to which a kid will go to make a statement of rebellion against his

Johnny's in the Basement revolves around the title character being pressured by his parents to let a few things go, including childish things, like the "World's Greatest Bottle Cap Collection," similar to the one pictured here.

family. *Johnny's in the Basement* is more realistic than *Sideways Stories from Wayside School*. Like many kids, Johnny learns that adults are not always in the right. Adults make mistakes, while children may sometimes have a better grasp on what's important in life.

WARNING: SMOKING INVOLVED!

Sachar included situations in *Johnny's in the Basement* that some adults found troubling. In particular, some critics and readers frowned about the inclusion of cigarette smoking in the book. According to Louissachar.com, in response to why he included an episode that depicted a health risk, especially in light of campaigns to persuade kids not to smoke, Sachar said, "When I was growing up, kids were very curious about cigarettes. We knew they were bad for us, but they didn't have the same sort of stigma as they have today. And so, kids would often experiment and try them. So, Donald experiments and tries cigarettes, as do Johnny and Valerie. But they're awful. It wasn't meant to encourage kids but to discourage them from trying cigarettes." The issue is a common one for authors (and all artists) who try to portray the truths about childhood and adolescence.

The scene did not hurt sales. *Johnny's in the Basement* became a best seller, earning Sachar praise from critics as well as a growing number of fans.

SOMEDAY ANGELINE

From a boy who collects bottle caps, Sachar turned to Angeline Persopolis, an eight-year-old with a high IQ who is the main protagonist in *Someday Angeline*, which was published in 1983. Angeline's intelligence is a mixed blessing. It makes her an object of torment for her class-mates. Even her teacher thinks she is a nuisance. To make matters worse, her father, a widower, does not know what to make of his bright and talented daughter. With the help of her friend Gary "Goon" Boone and a sympathetic teacher, Miss Turbone, Angeline learns how to be happy being herself. While some critics found the story uneven in its character-izations, others praised its themes of hope and acceptance.

A LIFE-CHANGING VISIT

By the time *Someday Angeline* was published, Sachar was receiving fan let-ters from kids all over the United States. He told *Texas Monthly*, "The first book [*Sideways Stories from Wayside School*] really hit in Texas... I got lots of mail from kids in Houston, Dallas, all over." Some of his biggest fans were the students at Davis Elementary School in Plano, who wrote to him regularly. They wanted him to visit their school. "Some of the girls had written things like, 'Our cute, single teacher thinks you're really great!'"

From the old days when he first began his career, and even through the modern era when most people would rather e-mail, Sachar has always enjoyed perusing through and responding to physical, handwritten fan mail.

Sachar finally accepted the invitation. He did think their teacher was very nice, but he found that he liked the school counselor, Carla Askew, even better. On May 26, 1985, Louis and Carla were married and moved into a small one-bedroom apartment in San Francisco.

Carla knew her husband wanted to quit the legal field and write full-time. In the *Horn Book Magazine*, she described her husband's struggle:

> When I met Louis, he was already a published author, had just passed the California bar exam, and was preparing his first court case. I learned very quickly that he had mixed feelings about what he really wanted to do with his life. He had just spent a lot of time and effort earning his law degree and knew he could probably support himself doing law work. He had also had the good fortune of having his first two books accepted for publication. Common sense told him he should proceed with his career as an attorney, but his heart pushed him to keep writing. Thank goodness his heart won the battle.

Not long after he met Carla, Louis Sachar decided to take the plunge and follow his dreams of writing full-time. After they married, Louis worked on his next book while Carla was at school. When not writing, he answered the many letters he received from children. Even during the summer when Carla had vacation, she left their tiny apartment so that Louis could work undisturbed. Carla believed deeply in her husband's talent and never once suggested that he go back to practicing law.

A STRANGELY SYMPATHETIC PROTAGONIST

Louis Sachar's fourth book took him longer to write than his previous titles. To complicate matters, he had trouble finding a publisher. Regardless of these difficulties, many critics agree that *There's a Boy in the Girls' Bathroom* (1987) is one of Sachar's best efforts. The story is about the transformation of the main character, Bradley Chalker, from a bully into a more sensitive and confident boy. In an interesting twist, Sachar tells Bradley's story from his point of view rather than that of his victims. Sachar denies that he drew from personal experience in his portrait of Bradley, about whom a critic noted in the *St. James Guide to Children's Writers*, "Sachar gives his reader the poignant and frequently unsettling opportunity to look through the eyes of a student whom every teacher dreads to see—a child to whom success, even if it were possible, would be terrifying."

Bradley Chalker is bright and imaginative. He is also the oldest student in the fifth-grade class at

Besides mere outcasts, some of Sachar's protagonists are even bullies or may be otherwise unsympathetic. Having them change throughout their narratives for the better is another Sachar touchstone.

Red Hill School, and he has earned a reputation for being a liar and a bully. Early on in the book, Sachar establishes Bradley's complete isolation from his classmates and his teacher:

> Bradley Chalker sat at his desk in the back of the room—last seat, last row. No one sat at the desk next to him or at the one in front of him. He was an island.

If he could have, he would have sat in the closet. Then he could shut the door so he wouldn't have to listen to Mrs. Ebbel. He didn't think she'd mind. She'd probably like it better that way too. So would the rest of the class. All in all, he thought everyone would be much happier if he sat in the closet, but unfortunately, his desk didn't fit.

When a new student, Jeff Fishkin, tries to befriend Bradley, Bradley is cruel to him:

"Hey, Bradley, wait up!" somebody called after him.

Startled, he turned around.

Jeff, the new kid, hurried alongside him. "Hi," said Jeff.

Bradley stared at him in amazement.

Jeff smiled. "I don't mind sitting next to you," he said. "Really."

Bradley didn't know what to say.

"I have been to the White House," Jeff admitted. "If you want, I'll tell you about it."

Bradley thought a moment, then said, "Give me a dollar or I'll spit on you."

Because the kids at school hate him, Bradley turns to his collection of chipped and broken pottery animals for comfort. Talking to them allows him to be all the things he cannot be with people: brave, smart, caring, and vulnerable. But Jeff Fishkin won't give up, and after mostly unpleasant encounters, the two boys gradually start to become friends.

There is another newcomer to Red Hill School, one who will play an even bigger role in Bradley's life. Carla, the new school counselor, known for the brightly colored shirts she wears, makes a point of seeking Bradley out. Carla's involvement with Bradley helps him to change his perspectives on things, especially himself. *There's a Boy in the Girls' Bathroom* tells a story of alienation and transformation. It also imparts the lesson that even non-sympathetic characters and people have more to them than initially meets the eye. Sachar's readers got the message that believing in yourself can often take some time and effort.

Sachar originally wanted the story to be told from two points of view: Bradley Chalker's and Jeff Fishkin's. His editors, however, thought the book would work better if the story was told from only Bradley's point of view. This meant several rewrites for Sachar. In creating the character of school counselor Carla Davis, Sachar borrowed his wife's first name and drew upon her experiences.

Another dilemma Sachar faced with the book was choosing a title. "The title is usually the last

Many writers experience writer's block, in which they are stumped in figuring out what happens next to their characters or storyline. Sachar does up to six drafts of a book and refuses to cave in to discouragement.

thing I think of," Sachar explained on Louissachar .com. "Although the whole time I'm writing the book, I'm trying to think of what I'll call it. But I discovered how important titles were with the success of *There's a Boy in the Girls' Bathroom*. Prior to that book, I hadn't been that successful. And that title got people to notice." For some critics, the title was a bit misleading. One reviewer for the *Bulletin of the Center for Children's Books* saw the book as "funny" but "not in the flip way implied by the title, but in the slightly sad sense that touches all true comedy."

Critics found much to like about *There's a Boy in the Girls' Bathroom*. *Kirkus Reviews* described it as the "fall and rise of Bradley Chalkers, class bully," while a review in *School Library Journal* raved that it was "unusual, witty, and satisfying." Young readers once more showed their loyalty, and the book soon appeared on reading lists at libraries and schools across the United States.

Louis Sachar's writing was becoming more thoughtful and serious, and *There's a Boy in the Girls' Bathroom* exemplified this shift. The lightweight storytelling that had proved such a successful formula with *Sideways Stories from Wayside School* was giving way to a deeper exploration into the world of preteens. Sachar was growing as a writer and expanding his ability to speak to young people in a language that was emotionally sincere.

A RISING STAR OF KIDS' FICTION

Now fully liberated from his day job, Sachar entered the late 1980s on a winning streak, fueled by creative growth and continuing success as a writer. He further explored the sensitive sides of believable preteen characters and captured the nuances of middle school behavior. Chief among his themes were acceptance and responsibility. He continued to make his mark with two new books during this time: *Sixth Grade Secrets*, which came out in 1987, and *The Boy Who Lost His Face*, published in 1989.

CHANGING DIRECTIONS

In 1987's *Sixth Grade Secrets*, eleven-year-old Laura Sibbie is the envy of her

classmates. One classmate, Gabriel, also has a crush on her. After finding a cap at a yard sale with the words "Pig City" written on it, Laura and her friends decide to form a secret club bearing the same name. To ensure that no one else finds out about the club, they each write down a secret, place it in a box, and agree never to talk about the club. If anyone breaks her promise, the other girls will reveal her secret to the entire school.

Throughout the book, Gabriel, Laura, and another classmate, Sheila, engage in

Sixth Grade Secrets deals with issues of rivalry, friendship, and secrecy. It is another work where the characters have to experience growing pains and rise above them.

middle-school bouts of competition and jealousy that are probably familiar to any sixth-grade reader. They play pranks and tricks, and they learn about betrayal and rivalry. One of the book's lessons is the length to which friends may inadvertently hurt each other and how they need to draw the lines that preserve privacy and maintain respect. The moral of the story is perhaps even more timely today, in an age of unending social media presence for many preteens.

MORE GROWING PAINS: *THE BOY WHO LOST HIS FACE*

In *The Boy Who Lost His Face* (1989), Sachar further explored the worries and fears of middle school students. The main character, David Ballinger, wants to be part of the popular crowd like his friend Scott. But David is afraid that he is too awkward to fit in. In an effort to be cool, David helps the group attack an elderly woman named Mrs. Bayfield, who, according to his new friends, is a witch who steals people's faces. During the attack (in which David takes away Mrs. Bayfield's cane), Mrs. Bayfield puts a curse on David.

At first, David thinks that this is nonsense. But odd things soon begin to happen to him. He falls backward in his chair during class and forgets to zip up his pants before Spanish class. He begins to believe that she really has cursed him. After more strange things occur, David decides to confront Mrs. Bayfield herself. The book humorously shows how young people are sometimes desperate enough for acceptance that they will do almost anything.

Eventually, David learns the importance of being true to himself and accepting responsibility for his actions. He struggles to redeem himself, though not without suffering some bumps and bruises along the way. One lesson Sachar imparts in this book is that people's real friends will accept them the way they are and pretending to be someone else always seems to backfire.

With *The Boy Who Lost His Face*, Sachar's writing moved farther away from the silly and gentle humor that marked his earlier work. At the heart of this story, however, are the themes that Sachar has visited again and again: the quest for identity and acceptance and the often bumpy transition from childhood to adolescence. For the first time, Sachar employed mature language and situations. The characters swear, and the attack on an elderly woman marked a rather violent turn for Sachar's subject matter. His editors were worried. In fact, they convinced him to tone down some of the language. Speaking about his decision to incorporate profanity and his reasons for removing some of the offensive words, Sachar noted in the anthology, *UXL Junior DISCovering Authors*:

> Initially the book had the 'f' word in it. My
> editor approved it, knowing full well I don't use
> words indiscriminately [randomly], but right
> before the book was published, a consultant
> informed me that if I didn't take it out, I'd be
> killing the sales of the book, as well as hurt
> my other books, and possibly kill my career in

The Albert Britnell Book Shop in Toronto, Ontario, displays a set of books that have been targets of banning and censorship efforts. Sachar has encountered criticism when it comes to controversial content.

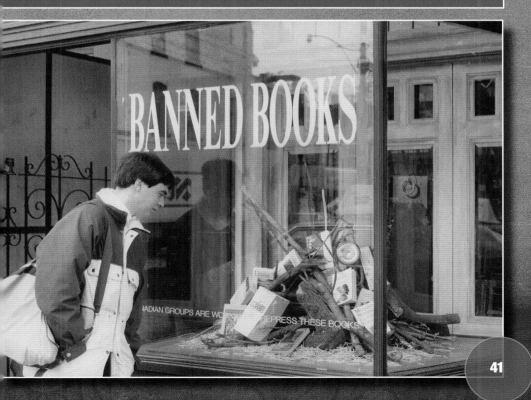

the process. Every single word in my books is important to me; however, I also know that kids don't worry about individual words as much when they're reading as I do when I'm writing. Although I believed the word belonged where I had put it, I agreed to change the text, because it would not ultimately affect how readers responded to the book. I find it very interesting that what people often object to is the word itself, rather than to content. As much as I might back down and change a word, I would never consider altering the moral or political content of a story.

THE WINNING *WAYSIDE* FORMULA

Although Sachar continued to experiment in his writing, the combination of letters from his young fans and the difficulty he had finding a publisher for *There's a Boy in the Girls' Bathroom* convinced him to return to Wayside School for his next book. In 1989, he published *Wayside School Is Falling Down*, a sequel to *Sideways Stories from Wayside School*. In *Falling Down*, fans of the first Wayside book welcomed the return of the students from Mrs. Jewl's class, who participate in a variety of zany antics, including a lesson in gravity that involves Mrs. Jewl dropping a classroom computer out a window.

Sachar explores the themes of self-awareness, identity, and popularity in *Wayside School Is Falling Down*. This time, he tackles serious themes with a lighter touch than in *The Boy Who Lost His Face*. In *Falling Down*, Benjamin Nushmutt, a new student to Mrs. Jewl's class, is mistakenly introduced as another student named Mark Miller. But before Benjamin can tell Mrs. Jewl about her mistake, he has become known as Mark Miller. The character's experiences as someone else end up providing unique insights, too. New identities allow for different behaviors and can thus be liberating. Being someone else can therefore be a great path to truly discovering who you are. Benjamin discovers that this new identity allows him to act differently, and he rather enjoys the change. It also helps him appreciate everyone else's differences, too. At one point he utters that he is "proud to be in a class where nobody was strange because nobody was normal."

Critics praised *Wayside School Is Falling Down*. The short chapters added to the book's appeal by making it easy for teachers to read aloud, just as they had done with the first Wayside book. Continuing with the successful Wayside School novels, Sachar published *Sideways Arithmetic from Wayside School* (1989), in which he indulged his love of mathematics by creating a collection of math puzzles. According to *UXL Junior DISCovering*

Authors, Sachar has this to say about the unique aspect of this installment in the series:

> While working on *There's a Boy in the Girls' Bathroom*, I wrote for about two hours every morning, and then every afternoon I made up a puzzle for the sequel to *Sideways Stories* entitled *Sideways Arithmetic from Wayside School*. Having enjoyed math so much when I was in grade school, I wanted

One of the spin-offs of his popular series, *Sideways Artithmetic from Wayside School,* was inspired by Sachar's childhood love of math, a subject that intimidates many students.

Sideways Arithmetic to help kids discover that math could be fun. Unfortunately, I think a lot of kids flip through the book, see all the puzzles, and automatically assume it will be too difficult, so they don't even attempt it. When I visit schools and put the first puzzle on the board, I ask the often lost-looking class to help solve it. Receiving little or no response, I go through it aloud, showing them step by step. When the next problem goes up on the board, kids start shouting answers.

Later, in 1995, Sachar returned to Wayside School one more time, writing *Wayside School Gets a Little Stranger*, a collection of thirty stories revolving around Mrs. Jewl's maternity leave.

INTRODUCING: MARVIN REDPOST

In 1992, Sachar introduced his fans to a new character, Marvin Redpost, a nine-year-old redhead who lives near Washington, D.C. In *Marvin Redpost: Kidnapped at Birth?* (1992), Marvin convinces himself that he is a long-lost prince who was stolen from his real parents, the king and queen of Shampoon, and was adopted by the Redpost family. In this book and its sequels, Sachar reexamines the theme of identity. Written for an audience of younger readers, the Redpost books also explore the importance of friendship and education. Adding to the books' appeal are their short chapters filled with fast-paced dialogue and comic situations.

During the next several years, Sachar wrote a number of Redpost books. In *Marvin Redpost: Is He a Girl?* (1993), Sachar pokes fun at the gender stereotypes associated with boys and girls. He addresses social taboos in *Marvin Redpost: Why Pick on Me?* (1993), a book in which Marvin

Pet cemeteries are one way for kids to deal with death. A pet dies under the care of the main character in *Marvin Redpost: Alone in His Teacher's House.*

becomes an outcast after being falsely accused of picking his nose.

Sachar's book *Marvin Redpost: Alone in His Teacher's House* (1994) takes on a weightier subject: death. When his teacher asks Marvin to take care of his aging dog, Waldo, Marvin is the envy of his friends. But when Waldo dies while in Marvin's care, he is overcome by feelings of guilt and grief, even though the death was not his fault. Marvin has to deal with the repercussions of the dog's death, including how his schoolmates react, while also trying to cope with his feelings and not fail his classes.

Sachar treats the relationship between youngsters and animals with sensitivity. Ultimately, this title in the Redpost series broadly tackles issues such as self-pity, selflessness, and empathy.

GARY "GOON" BOONE

In between working on the Marvin Redpost books, Sachar returned to coming-of-age stories. In *Dogs Don't Tell Jokes* (1991), Gary "Goon" Boone (who first appears in *Someday Angeline*) is a compulsive joke-teller who thinks all of his jokes are hysterical. However, they aren't.

Gary, who is in the seventh grade, dreams of becoming a stand-up comic. The problem is that he is not funny. As a result, almost everyone finds him

A FAMILY MAN

Big changes were afoot for the Sachars by the end of the 1980s. In 1987, they had their first and only child, a daughter they named Sherre. They were also on the cusp of a big relocation. By 1990, *There's a Boy in the Girls' Bathroom* had won several prizes, including the Texas Bluebonnet Award. Shortly after traveling to Texas to accept the award, the Sachars decided to leave San Francisco and move to Austin.

Luckily, having a child didn't mean that Louis had no time to write. To make sure her husband had the quiet time he needed, Carla dropped Sherre off at the babysitter's before going to work. At home, Louis wrote in the mornings and answered letters or did research in the afternoons. Before Carla and Sherre returned home, he cleaned up his materials and put the house in order.

Sherre has even had an impact on her father's writing, both as a sometime adviser and as an inspiration for characters. The one-year-old sister in *The Boy Who Lost His Face* and Marvin Redpost's sister were both inspired by Sherre. Once she was old enough to read his work, she provided valuable feedback. Along with Carla, she is the first to see his books before anyone else.

tiresome. When a talent show with a $100 prize is announced at school, Gary is convinced his moment has arrived. He decides to enter, but his parents have an alternate plan in mind. They promise to give him $100 if he stops telling jokes for three weeks. Gary accepts his parents' proposition only to find that not telling jokes proves to be harder than he imagined. He looks into other hobbies and pursuits but misses comedy fiercely.

One of the main messages of *Dogs Don't Tell Jokes* is that it is not enough to call yourself a comedian. As with any craft or art, it takes hard work, practice, and sacrifice. Being able to tell what is funny to others can take time. The book is really about Gary's growth, both as a comedian and a person who takes criticism and uses it to improve. As with many of Sachar's other works, it is also about a protagonist's search for his identity and quest for happiness.

By the time he published *Dogs Don't Tell Jokes*, Sachar had a reputation as one of the most talented and incisive children's writers of the 1980s and 1990s. But it was a vacation outing to Maine and the hot summers of Texas that inspired Sachar to produce his best known, best selling, and perhaps most beloved work.

HOLES

In 1995, the Sachars traveled to Maine to escape the oppressive heat of Texas in the summer. While there, Sachar worked on an entirely new and different project: a book for adults. He had started it nearly two years earlier and had played with it and off. He could never truly get the book off the ground, however. He never felt the plot and characters were developed enough.

Sachar finally realized that it was no use to continue and abandoned the manuscript. He and his family returned to Austin, where the hot summer lingered. Sachar hates the summer heat, especially the summer heat in Texas. As Carla noted in the *Horn Book Magazine*, the climate there made it difficult to even venture outside. "Often just walking out of the air-conditioned house into a summer day can take your breath away."

Sachar added, "There are no breaks from the Texas summer heat. It starts, if we're lucky, in late May, and continues until almost Halloween. September and October are the worst. In July and August you expect it to be hot. That's part of the bargain. But then it just keeps going on, week after week, while you know that in other parts of the country people are enjoying crisp fall air and colorful leaves." Little did Sachar know that hardship would soon spark creative inspiration. His loathing of the heat would be just the thing to encourage him to write his newest book.

Sachar was ready for a new challenge. As he recalled to *Instructor* magazine, "I had already written lots of books about kids in school. I wanted to do something completely different. I was sick of school. It was August, and the weather was hot, and I got the idea to write about

The South Congress district of Austin, Texas, is a popular place for shopping, going out, and dining.

A group of female juvenile offenders at a boot camp stand at attention. A similar but fictional detention center provided the unusual setting for *Holes*, Sachar's most well-known work.

a juvenile correctional facility, a boot camp for 'bad boys,' where the boys were required to dig holes, every day, under the brutal Texas sun."

For the next year and a half, Sachar wrote and wrote. From the outset, he was aware that the book he was writing was different from anything he had done before. For one thing, he always began writing with a specific character in mind. However, this time he didn't have one. Instead, he was inspired by a setting, a place that he called Camp Green Lake, even though there was no lake and nothing green anywhere in sight. He explained how the book began to unfold in a later speech:

> Every day I would begin by turning on my computer and typing the word "try." This turned out to be very helpful, psychologically. *Holes* was the most ambitious book I'd ever tried to write. There were times when it seemed hopeless, when the story got so bogged down that I didn't think I could ever make it work—and this after spending two years on a novel that I'd never finished. So it was very comforting to begin each day by telling myself just to try.

Sachar later admitted in an interview with Scholastic that he "didn't know what was going to happen there, or even who the main character would be . . . [but] the place seemed ripe for a story." The book took off from there. Sachar, in an awards speech later, laid out the creative train of thought that yielded some of the skeleton of the plot of *Holes*:

> Perhaps it was a result of the frustration of having worked two years on a novel that

Sachar is shown onstage giving his speech accepting his National Book Award for *Holes* on Novemeber 18, 1998, in New York City. It is one of many honors the book has received over the years.

lacked strong characters and plot. As soon as I came up with the idea that the juvenile inmates of Camp Green Lake would be required to dig holes, almost immediately I had the idea that there would be buried treasure somewhere out there. I decided it was buried by a famous outlaw named Kissin' Kate Barlow, although I didn't know anything about her yet, and I decided that the warden would be the granddaughter of Kate Barlow, who was using the juvenile delinquents as slave labor to look for her grandmother's buried treasure. And I made up the deadly yellow-spotted lizards, lurking somewhere out there, although I didn't know what I'd do with them yet.

THE UNLUCKY HERO OF *HOLES*

Holes is the story of Stanley Yelnats, an overweight kid with no friends and even less luck. He gets teased in school and lives in an apartment that smells like dirty feet. To make matters worse, Stanley suffers from a family curse that began with his great-great-grandfather, Elya Yelnats. When Stanley is wrongfully accused of stealing a pair of sneakers, he has a choice: go to jail or go to Camp Green Lake, an institution for wayward boys, where the strange philosophy of rehabilitation is "If you take a bad boy and make him dig a hole every day in the hot sun, it will turn him into a good boy."

Stanley blames his latest streak of bad luck on his "no-good-dirty-rotten-pig-stealing-great-great-grandfather," whose failure to honor a promise to an old gypsy woman named Madame Zeroni began the family's history of misfortune.

A villainous female warden operates Camp Green Lake. She keeps her charges in line with fingernails that are polished with rattlesnake venom. One scratch of the nails and the unlucky inmate is poisoned. The warden also forces the inmates to dig holes, each one approximately 5 feet (1.5 meters) deep and 5 feet across. If the boys find anything in the course of their digging, they are to report immediately to the warden.

When taken to the work area, Stanley sees a landscape "so full of holes and mounds that it reminded him of pictures he'd seen of the moon." Day after day, as Stanley digs, he begins to wonder if in fact there isn't something buried in the sand. When Stanley does discover the truth, he unknowingly sets into motion a series of events that will fulfill his destiny, bringing the past and present together.

Sachar had two big problems writing *Holes*, as he told the *Austin Chronicle*: "I wanted to put the background in about Stanley's great-great-grandfa-ther, and I didn't want to just all of a sudden in the middle of the story just go, 'Okay, now here's what happened to Stanley's great-great-grandfather.'" The other problem was how to keep readers inter-ested in Stanley and the hole digging without getting repetitive: "I wanted the reader to feel what a long, miserable experience this is, digging those 5' by 5' holes. But how many times can you say, 'He dug his shovel back into the dirt and lifted out another shovelful?'"

Sachar solved the problem by interweaving the story of Stanley at Camp Green Lake with the story of his great-great-grandfather. Added to the story line is the fact that while Stanley knows some of his family's history, the reader often finds out more before he does or even at the same time as Stanley. Sachar's use of alternating between the past and the present keeps the pace moving and readers on their toes. As each piece of the puzzle falls into place, Stanley's quest to break the family curse becomes ever more urgent.

By connecting the two stories, Sachar shows that history repeats itself. Just like Stanley, Elya Yelnats was in the wrong place at the wrong time. As a result, he ran afoul of Kissin' Kate Barlow, the ruthless Texas outlaw. Sachar structured Kate's and Elya's story to parallel Stanley's. Though the novel may seem a bit haphazard in the beginning, the two story lines come together to lead to a rousing climax.

One of the most successful aspects of *Holes* comes from Sachar's use of folkloric devices. One was a make-believe lullaby sung by different generations of the Yelnats family. The repetition of such elements helped unite the story lines.

In addition, Sachar's repetition of themes and phrases throughout the book, such as his description of Stanley's friend Zero ("Zero said nothing"), resonated with readers and critics alike. When Zero finally does say something, it is crucial to the story's plot.

DIGGING UP A BREAKTHROUGH

Sachar gave the manuscript of *Holes* to his eight-year-old daughter, Sherre, to read. She pointed out the parts of the book that worked and the parts that didn't. As with *There's a Boy in the Girls' Bathroom*, Sachar had a hard time coming up with a good title. He didn't really like the proposed title, *Holes*, and thought instead of going with the one that he and Sherre liked best: *Wrong Place, Wrong Time, Wrong Kid*.

In the end, though, *Holes* won out. Sachar also decided to keep Stanley's last name, explaining later that he "came up with the name Stanley Yelnats because [he] didn't feel like figuring out a last name." As he told Scholastic.com, "I just spelled his last name backwards and figured I'd change it later. But I didn't." Sachar created one of his most memorable characters in Stanley, the luck-less boy whose name is a palindrome.

Based on his daughter's recommendations and his own need to revise the text, Sachar did another draft of the manuscript. In all, he wrote five drafts of *Holes* before he was satisfied enough with it to send it out. *Holes* was published in 1998. The book became a huge success with readers of all ages and received universal praise from reviewers and critics. A *Publishers Weekly* review called it a "dazzling blend of social commentary, tall tale and magic realism," and found it to be "a wry [clever] and loopy novel."

It seemed that tons of young readers identified with Stanley, a fact that wasn't that surprising to Sachar, who explained to Scholastic.com:

> Stanley isn't a hero-type. He's kind of a pathetic kid who feels like he has no friends, feels like his life is cursed. And I think everyone can identify with that in one way or another. And then the fact that here he is, a kid who isn't a hero—he rises and becomes

one. I think people can see themselves rising with Stanley.

Holes marked another departure for Sachar. It is a much darker, much scarier, and more disturbing work than his previous efforts. Even Sachar's daughter found the character of the warden frightening, though Sachar says he was surprised by Sherre's response. To him, the warden—with her rattlesnake-venom fingernails—was, as he told the

A dry lake bed in an arid landscape is reminiscent of the the setting of *Holes*. One main influence for this fictional environment was the unforgiving heat of Texas, which Sachar despised.

Austin Chroncile, "almost cartoonish . . . like a character in Batman or something."

In June 2002, one thousand young-adult readers
selected *Holes* to receive the first annual Readers'
Choice Award for Teen Books, presented by *Read*
magazine. *Read* is a literary magazine for grades
six through ten and is published by Weekly Reader.
The award, established in honor of *Read* magazine's

HOLES MAKES HISTORY

Among the biggest surprises for Sachar was the
announcement in February 1999 that *Holes* had won
the Newbery Medal—the highest honor a children's
author can win in the United States. Sachar was
"amazed" when he heard the news, and he recalled
the phone call in his acceptance speech: "I was awak-
ened by a phone call at seven o'clock in the morning
on February 1 and was told the great news. I could
tell I was on a speakerphone, and I knew they were
eagerly awaiting my reaction. I felt I was letting
everyone down by not screaming. Sorry." Sachar also
joked in his speech that the pressure of writing the
acceptance speech was greater than that of actually
writing the book.

Holes also won the prestigious National Book
Award in 1998. This put Sachar in the literary history
books. That is because he was the first author ever to
win both awards for the same book.

fiftieth anniversary, is the first of its kind. Although there are many state awards programs that involve a student selection committee, the Readers' Choice Award is the first and only national award for which the nominees and the winners are chosen entirely by students. Competition for the award was tough and included popular children's authors such as Christopher Paul Curtis (*The Watsons Go to Birmingham*, 1995), Richard Peck (*A Year Down Yonder*, 2000), J. K. Rowling (*Harry Potter and the Goblet of Fire*, 2000), and Jerry Spinelli (*Stargirl*, 2000).

While prestigious awards and the recognition that comes with winning them can be enjoyable, they are certainly not the most important thing in Louis Sachar's life. You can tell by what he says when questioned about his status as a recognized author. In an interview he gave after winning the Newbery Medal, Sachar told Scholastic.com, "Well, I suppose it's nice to get recognition from people who matter. In a sense." When an interviewer from *Book Report* asked him if fan letters and awards from children outweigh the honor of winning national awards, Sachar replied simply, "They're both nice." When the interviewer followed up with a question about the possibility of *Holes* being made into a movie, Sachar remained unflappable, saying, "I try not to get too excited."

SACHAR ON THE SILVER SCREEN

Regardless of how much he downplayed his success, Sachar had good reason to be excited. Teresa
Tucker-Davies, a producer for the Chicago Pacific
Entertainment Company, came across a synopsis of
Holes and knew immediately that she had just found
her next film project. The company bought the film
rights, and director Andrew Davis, who also headed

Young actor and future star Shia LaBeouf made his major cinematic debut in the 2003 film
version of *Holes* playing the title character of Stanley Yelnats. Despite production issues, the
adaptation was well-regarded by audiences and critics.

Chicago Pacific Entertainment, signed on to direct. Never for a moment did Sachar think that the producers or the director would want him to write the screenplay. He believed they would hire someone with more experience. However, during one meeting, as Sachar recalled to *Publishers Weekly*, "They turned to me and said, 'How about you?'"

Finding actors to fill the roles of the book's characters proved more challenging than expected. Andrew Davis admitted to *Publishers Weekly*, "It was harder on Louis than us to cast the boys—he'd lived with the characters in his head for so long." Sachar added, "We didn't want TV commercial actors . . . We needed slightly goofy kids." The cast included Shia LaBeouf as Stanley, Sigourney Weaver as the warden, and Henry Winkler as Stanley's father. Sachar himself even had a small cameo role as a shopkeeper in the town of Green Lake.

Working on the film version of *Holes* gave Sachar a firsthand view of how films are made. In an interview he gave while on the set, Sachar said, "Everyone thinks that writing a screenplay is just dialogue. But it's not. It's making things visual."

Sachar has learned a great deal from his experience. "Now that I've seen the work out here, I think I'd be better at it. I watch movies differently now," he told *Publishers Weekly*.

HOLES, THE MOVIE

Holes the film came out in April 2003 and, for the most part, won over both critics and audiences, doing very well at the box office and among movie reviewers. Roger Ebert of the *Chicago Sun-Times* wrote that he "walked in expecting a movie for thirteensomethings, and walked out feeling challenged and satisfied," adding that "it was grown up and sophisticated."

While he was generally satisfied with the screen version of *Holes*, Sachar had more ambivalent feelings toward the production process involved in making the film. The initial development process took about three years and was a whirlwind for the author and his story. Sachar felt nervous when he lost control of the final story once he sold the movie rights, even though he was enlisted to write the screenplay.

He told the *New York Times* in 2006, "The movie had several producers along with their staff, all looking at the material for the first time, and saying how things should be changed, often not even realizing the effects of all their changes. There were times when the screenplay (which I wrote) had been so badly altered, and in my mind, distorted, that I contemplated taking my name off of it. Fortunately I had a very good relationship with the director, who would always listen to my protests, and by the time the movie was shot, most of the things I really felt strongly about were fixed."

In retrospect, Sachar is unsure whether he did the best he could have done with *Holes*, although he felt good about the book when he sent it to his publisher. "I get a real clear vision at different parts of a book," he told the *Austin Chronicle*. "I know what I'm going to do here. And then I get kind of lost. I'm always amazed when I finish a book and realize, 'Hey this is actually what I set out to do.'"

STANLEY YELNATS' SURVIVAL GUIDE TO CAMP GREEN LAKE

Partially to capitalize on the wave of anticipation accompanying the release of the motion picture version of *Holes* in 2003, and partly out of a tongue-in-cheek creative inspiration, Sachar wrote a companion book to *Holes*. Released in March 2003, *Stanley Yelnats' Survival Guide to Camp Green Lake* was not a sequel per se but did provide more insight into the world that Sachar had constructed. As the title indicates, it is a funny handbook on how to survive and even thrive at the fictional Camp Green Lake. According to Louissachar.com, "Should you ever find yourself at Camp Green Lake—or somewhere similar—this is the guide for you. Stanley (Caveman, to some of you) offers anecdotes and advice on everything from digging the perfect hole to identifying and avoiding the wildlife (scorpions, tarantulas, rattlesnakes, yellow-spotted lizards, Mr. Sir) to help make your stay a more pleasant one."

SMALL STEPS: THE *HOLES* SAGA CONTINUES

After the more tongue-in-cheek release of the second book in the series, Sachar dove back into the universe he created for *Holes* and began work on a follow-up. It would take him some time and would actually have less in common with the previous novel than readers expected.

In fact, some of the inspiration for *Small Steps*, eventually published in January 2006, arose from the initially troubled script process for *Holes* the movie back in 2003. At the time, Sachar fantasized about two minor characters from the first novel, Theodore "Armpit" Johnson and Rex "X-Ray" Washburn, being so upset with their characters' portrayal by Hollywood that they would travel to Los Angeles to demand compensation. This seed of an idea grew into a plot that relocated these same characters, whom Sachar had grown to be fond of, to his native Austin, Texas. The book's title refers to Armpit's small steps to transcend his past as a juvenile offender and graduate high school, get a job and save money, avoid violence and crime, and move beyond his unfortunate nickname. An illegal ticket scalping scheme thought up by Rex threatens to derail his plans, however, and their further misadventures suck in his ten-year-old friend Ginny and a teen singing sensation named Kaira DeLeon.

As in *Holes*, some of the adult characters in *Small Steps* manage to come off worse and more ruthless than Sachar's younger protagonists. Sachar told the *New York Times* he was not trying to replicate *Holes*, nor even write a true sequel. He noted, "I wanted to write a story addressing problems faced by an African-American teenager, especially one with a criminal record . . . [The] story stands very much on its own." Despite its differences with its predecessor, *Small Steps* nonetheless offers similar lessons in resilience and redemption and defying the expectations of others, including society at large.

Sachar has been asked countless times what theme or message he hoped to convey in *Holes*. In his acceptance speech for the Newbery Medal, he pointed out that he "didn't write the book for the purpose of teaching kids that something their great-great-grandparents did long ago might have cursed them." He continued, "I included the curse only because I think most adolescents can identify with the feeling that their lives must be cursed. The book was written for the sake of the book, and nothing beyond that. If there's any lesson at all, it is that reading is fun."

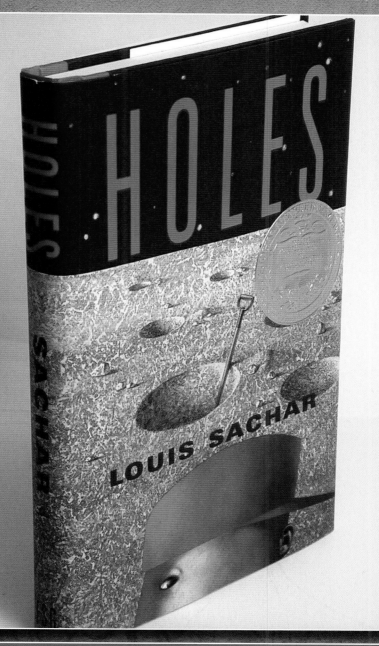

An edition of *Holes* bears the distinctive Newbery Medal stamp on its cover. *Holes* won in 1999, and Sachar thus joined the company of authors such as Beverly Cleary, Lloyd Alexander, and Lois Lowry.

A book need not be preachy to make someone a better person, he believes. Sachar feels that books help young people in more roundabout ways, even if they do not explicitly teach a reader specific morals. Simply sitting down and reading, and thus getting into the world of a character and his or her fears, hopes, and struggles, provides a lesson in empathy. Readers can thus develop skills they hopefully carry on into adulthood, along with a love of books.

A WRITER
AT WORK

Every writer has his or her own ways of approaching the creative process. The rules and rituals writers rely on are as many and varied as there are writers out there. For many, it is important to maintain a routine. This gives them the structure they require to separate from all other activities and pressures and concentrate on their work.

Like any author, Louis Sachar has his own daily schedule, including a writing routine. He starts every day in basically the same way. He showers and dresses before making his way to the kitchen, where he drinks a glass of freshly squeezed grapefruit juice, boils water for his morning cup of tea, and makes his breakfast. He then reads the morning paper, making sure to

CHAPTER

FIVE

71

A player holds a hand while playing bridge, a popular card game that remains one of Sachar's most beloved hobbies and was a big part of his 2010 work, *The Cardturner.*

work on the daily bridge column. Louis rarely chats over breakfast. On work days, as soon as he is finished eating, he's off to write. He relocates to the study, which is located in a room above the garage.

A DAILY ROUTINE

As soon as the door to Sachar's office is closed, it is a signal to everyone in the house that he is at work and

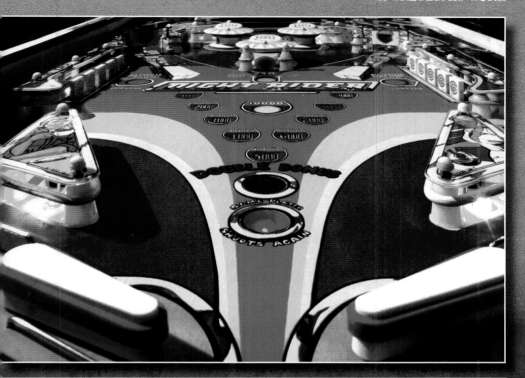

A close-up of a vintage pinball machine is shown here. Once popular in arcades, pinball declined with the rise of video games. Nowadays, pinball machines can be found in the houses of fans like Louis Sachar, who plays daily.

should remain undisturbed. Sometimes, when Sachar is just beginning a new book, the house will be filled with the sounds of his pinball machine (located in his office) as he takes a break to think things over.

Sachar follows a strict work regime. He writes on a computer using an old program called Wordstar, which does not require a mouse or a version of Windows to operate. Sachar discussed his method of writing with Scholastic.com:

I write every morning. After about two hours, I can feel myself losing energy and concentration. It's best to quit when I'm still excited about what I'm writing. Then I'll be ready to go when I start the next day. I couldn't write for a longer amount of time, even if I wanted to. Tippy has gotten used to my schedule, and after two hours she taps me with her paw, howls, barks, and otherwise lets me know it's time for her walk.

Sometimes when working on a first draft, Sachar may work only forty-five minutes each day. Then he lets the draft sit for twenty-four hours and returns to it the next day. To keep the process moving along, he gives his computer files some interesting names. During the writing of *Holes*, for instance, Sachar called some of his early files "NowWhat" and "AndThen" because he was unsure what would happen next as he wrote.

Sachar writes five days a week. When asked what he likes most about writing, he told Scholastic .com, "I think it's [the] tremendous feeling of accomplishment that I get from starting with nothing, and somehow creating a whole story and setting and characters."

But Sachar added that there's also a downside. Referring to what he likes least about writing he said:

Most days, it just feels like I'm not accomplishing much . . . most of it just seems like a waste of time. It amazes me how after a year, all those wasted days somehow add up to nothing. Another thing I don't like is that it's a very solitary profession. I think it would be nice sometimes to go to an office and see people every day, instead of just sitting in my room.

While Sachar reserves the mornings for writing, he devotes his afternoons to answering the letters he receives from young fans. As his success and fame have grown, writing a personal response to every correspondent has become more difficult. His wife Carla told the *Horn Book Magazine*, "The letters may sit in a pile on the floor across from his desk for weeks at a time, [but Louis] always takes time to personally answer all of the mail from his readers . . . Each child is important to him, so he is determined to give them all the respect they deserve."

WORKS IN PROGRESS: UNDER WRAPS

There is one other important rule in the Sachar household. Sachar makes it a practice to never discuss his work in progress because, as he told the *Horn Book Magazine*, "By working on a book for a year without talking about it—even to my wife—the story keeps building inside, until it's bursting to be told and the words come pouring out when I sit down to write." Sachar's daughter, Sherre, added that her father's rule on this was "one of my dad's toughest." She and her mother might know only that her father's current project is a Marvin Redpost book or another Wayside School book. Sherre also said her father "doesn't want anyone giving him suggestions; he says it interferes with his creative process."

For Carla and Sherre, the wait is worth it. When Sachar finishes a manuscript, he lets them read it. As Sherre described it to the *Horn Book Magazine*, "We both love the day when Dad says, 'OK, my book is finished. Anyone want to read it?'" Sherre will tell her dad when there's something that might be hard for kids to understand, while Carla looks for errors. Sachar always wants lots of feedback at this point before he begins to rework the material.

Sachar admits he wasn't sure how having a family would affect his writing. He told *UXL Junior DISCovering Authors*, "When I first started writing, I spent a great deal of time alone. Solitude allowed me to think about a project at all times—even when not actually writing—and I was afraid that with someone else around, I'd lose valuable thinking time. But family life has given me a sense of stability [that] has improved my writing rather than hindered

Sachar continues to challenge himself and work hard well into his fourth decade of writing. Having a routine and balancing work, family, and other activities helps keep this popular author going.

it." It helps, too, that both Carla and Sherre recognize Sachar's needs and are more than willing to make adjustments.

THE IDEA FACTORY

Like any writer, Sachar has his own way to deal with problems that occur. His brainstorming process can lead from one idea to the next, and it is not always the first or second idea that proves viable for a story. He sometimes begins a book and works on it for a time before abandoning it for another story idea entirely. While working on a first draft, Sachar rarely if ever knows what will happen further along in the story, much less how it will end. Sometimes this results in very disorganized narratives that he must rewrite several times. Writing is not always easy, and Sachar sometimes looks back on a project as being more fun than it actually was.

The amount of time it takes Sachar to write a book varies from project to project. For example, books in the Marvin Redpost series can take anywhere from four to six months to complete, while Sachar spent more than eighteen months writing *Holes.*

Almost every new project begins the same way. Sachar spends about a month brainstorming before he begins to sketch out ideas for characters and a plot. His early efforts, though, are often premature, leading to many false starts and dead ends. As he explained in his Newbery speech, "I'll get an idea, write a few words on my computer, think 'That's stupid!' and delete it. I'll try something else—'That's dumb!'—and try again." Sometimes, though, the process works in reverse, and Sachar returns to ideas he discarded earlier. "I'll get an idea that may not seem very special at first; however, as I write, it immediately starts to grow. One idea leads to another idea, and that idea leads to another idea . . . until I have a story going."

Like many writers, Sachar often battles writer's block. Usually he will force himself to write anything in order to get through it. Because he does on average anywhere from four to six drafts of a book, he can work through any technical problems. When he is satisfied that he has an acceptable manuscript, he sends a copy to his publisher (Sachar has had different publishers for his books), but at that point the manuscript is far from done. Sachar works with his editor to revise it, which usually means he will do additional drafts before the manuscript is ready for publication.

When it comes to discussing his own books and future projects, Sachar is quite thoughtful. He views his books on the Wayside School as fantasy and believes that it is far more difficult to write realistic works such as *There's a Boy in the Girls' Bathroom*. When asked about the differences, Sachar said in *UXL Junior DISCovering Authors*, "When you write something like *Sideways Stories*, people tend to say, 'What an imagination it takes to think of all those fantastical things.' On the contrary, I think it takes a greater imagination to write realistic stories complete with realistic details. It's simple to invent, but to get to the heart of reality takes some real creativity."

One thing he does not think about when writing is the moral or lesson to be learned in his books. In his Newbery Medal acceptance speech, he stated, "It's hard to imagine anyone asking an author of an adult novel what morals or lessons he or she was trying to teach the reader. But there is a perception that if you write for young people, then the book should be a lesson of some sort, a learning experience, a step toward something else." Sachar just wants kids to enjoy reading and perhaps to begin thinking about who they are and who they want to become.

Frances Foster, Sachar's editor at Farrar, Straus and Giroux, compared his success to that of Roald Dahl, the well-known and beloved author of *Charlie and the Chocolate Factory* (1964) and *James and the Giant Peach* (1961). "Louis was discovered by the children who loved his books, like the Wayside

School stories," Foster said. "There are books [that] adults discover and push onto kids—this was completely the other way around." In fact, Sachar's popularity with kids brought him to the notice of parents, teachers, librarians, and booksellers, and that popularity has translated into success.

Today, Sachar's books have become best sellers the world over, appearing in approximately twenty countries. About this international success, Sachar admitted, "It's fun to get these books published in different languages, even though I can't read them!"

According to Carla Sachar, there is another secret to Louis's success. In a piece written for the *Horn Book Magazine*, she described what she thought made her husband successful at writing for children: "Louis is a kid at heart. He loves playing games, being outside, and not working. (He doesn't consider writing 'work.') Children who read his books have either been through similar situations, hoped they would never go through anything like it, or have witnessed someone else living through it. His work crosses the boundaries of age and is enjoyed by young and old alike."

According to Carla, there is another reason why his books are so popular. She said many people have asked both of them how his depictions of children's feelings, attitudes, and actions are so often on the mark. Readers also wonder if the young

A young boy in a library reads a copy of *Sideways Stories from Wayside School*. The commitment of Sachar's diehard readers has helped ensure that he continues to publish and captivate his old fans and growing numbers of new fans worldwide.

characters are usually based on him or those he knew in childhood. Sachar insists that they are purely made up but that naturally elements of his own experience and his friends in childhood contribute to his characters' development. Rather, it is the universal experiences that all people have in childhood, he believes, that make their plights so recognizable.

A WORK/LIFE BALANCE

Louis Sachar has worked hard to balance work with leisure, family time, and other pursuits. When he is not writing, he takes long walks with his dogs, often in Carla's company. At various times, Sachar and his wife and daughter have been longtime volunteers at the Austin Society for the Prevention of Cruelty to Animals (SPCA), where have helped take care of homeless dogs. As for hobbies, Sachar enjoys skiing and tennis, but he reserves his greatest passion for bridge. He enjoys the mathematical aspect of the game and participates in duplicate bridge tournaments all across the country. He has even earned the title of "life master" for his expertise at the game.

Still as passionate about writing for young people as he was when he first started decades ago, Louis Sachar, according to Sherre's description in the *Horn Book Magazine*, sees himself as two different people: "a writer and a dad who just happens to have the exact same name." Sachar's own quirky personality has provided him with one of the most important and interesting themes of his work.

A WRITER FOR ALL AGES

When asked what advice he has for young writers, Sachar told the audience during his Newbery acceptance speech, "Read, find out what you like to read, and try to figure out what it is about it that makes you like it." In his opinion, writing for children is one of the toughest but most rewarding occupations a person can undertake. As for the secret of his own success, Sachar added, "I try to think of the world as a kid would see it. Then I write a story that I would like as an adult."

Frances Foster, Sachar's editor at Farrar, Straus and Giroux, the New York-based publisher, concurs that the writer challenges expectations people have about young-adult fiction. In an interview about Sachar, Foster said, "There's this . . . view that places children's literature below the literature written for adults. But when you think back through the ages, of what has been published for children, the really classic books have all had very high standards of plot and structure and characterization."

Sachar cites Kurt Vonnegut's *Hocus Pocus* (1990) and William Goldman's *The Princess Bride* (1987), for example, as influences on *Holes*. "I like the way the opening chapters were sort of short and jumpy," Sachar recalls, "and how they led into the story . . . And *The Princess Bride* had these colorful characters and this bizarre setting, and that's sort of like *Holes*."

It's important for writers to be aware of what others are doing in their field, and Sachar counts Katherine Paterson, Lois Lowry, Avi, and Walter Dean Myers as some of his favorite writers for young readers. He would like to try his hand at other types of stories, especially scary stories.

THE CARDTURNER

One of Sachar's talents has been the ability to mine entertaining stories from unusual sources. His 2010 novel, *The Cardturner*, has taken the coming-of-age story and incorporated one of Sachar's very favorite pastimes—playing bridge. Teenager Alton Richards is beginning an aimless summer vacation having been dumped by his girlfriend and still looking for a summer job. Alton's mother volunteers him to fill in as his blind uncle Lester's driver and cardturner for his bridge games. Unexpectedly, Alton bonds with his uncle while becoming a surprising success at bridge.

Alton narrates early on in the book, "I realize that reading about a bridge game isn't exactly thrilling." However, Sachar proves his own main character wrong in actually writing a briskly plotted and lively narrative with bridge as a main component. His curmudgeonly uncle gives him pointers on the game and life, and Alton's reflections as he interacts with his family and friends take him through a truly unexpected summer. As *Publishers Weekly* wrote, "Luckily, this funny and thoughtful novel is as much about building bridges—between generations and maybe even between life and death—as it is about playing cards."

The last decade and a half remained productive ones for Louis Sachar. In addition to two Marvin Redpost books released in 2000 (*Super Fast Out of Control!* and *A Magic Crystal?*), he released *Small Steps* in 2006.

FUZZY MUD...AND THE FUTURE

In 2015, Sachar published *Fuzzy Mud*. Part science fiction, part horror, the book is another tale of plucky, resourceful young people dealing with an adverse situation. In this case, fifth-grader Tamaya and her seventh-grade friend Marshall, while trying to avoid a school bully, come across a mysterious pool of mud in the woods. Their encounter with this mud sets off a fast-paced tale of apocalyptic disaster surrounding "frankengerms." Altogether, *Fuzzy Mud*, according to *Kirkus Reviews*, is an "exciting story of school life, friends, and bullies that becomes a quick meditation on the promise and dangers of modern science."

His output has not been limited to books and his sole screenplay for *Holes*. Sachar has also adapted two of his books, *There's a Boy in the Girls' Bathroom* and *Holes*, for the stage. But adapting a book to the stage proved more difficult than writing another book because, as Sachar says, it was "hard to generate the [creative] spark again."

Whatever narrative paths his future works take, Louis Sachar's career as a published author is nearly four decades long, and he shows no sign of stopping. His ability to tell a spellbinding tale while revealing the universal truths of childhood and adolescence remain a powerful draw for the millions who have fallen in love with Sachar's work.

ON LOUIS SACHAR

Birth date: March 10, 1954

Birthplace: East Meadow, New York

Parents: Robert Sachar, father, and Ruth Raybin Sachar, mother.

Current home: Austin, Texas

First Publication: *Sideways Stories from Wayside School* (1978, Wilcox & Follett)

Education:

University of California, Berkeley, Bachelor of Arts in Economics, 1976

University of California, Hastings College of the Law, Juris Doctor (law degree), 1980

Spouse: Carla Sachar, nee Askew, married 1985

Children: One daughter, Sherre Sachar, born 1989

Hobbies: Bridge, especially duplicate bridge; pinball; skiing

Favorite authors: Margaret Atwood, E. L. Doctorow, Kazuo Ishiguro, Richard Price, J. D. Salinger, Kurt Vonnegut, E. B White.

ON LOUIS SACHAR'S WORK

Johnny's in the Basement, Alfred A. Knopf/Avon Books, 1981

Title character Johnny faces growing up by hunkering down in his basement with the world's greatest bottle cap collection. His parents' ultimatum to get rid of his collection and try to embrace the world somehow ends up in dance lessons and his fateful meeting with the friend that will change his life, fellow dance student Valerie.

There's a Boy in the Girls' Bathroom, Alfred A. Knopf, 1987

School misfit and bully Bradley Chalkers has the worst reputation in his school and seems to prefer it that way. He is challenged to re-examine this reputation and show a little bit of his true self.

Awards: Georgia Children's Book Award; Iowa Children's Choice Award; Nevada Young Reader's Award; Texas Bluebonnet Award

The Boy Who Lost His Face, Alfred A. Knopf, 1989

Dogs Don't Tell Jokes, Alfred A. Knopf, 1991

Monkey Soup, Alfred A. Knopf, 1992

Holes, Farrar, Strauss and Giroux, 1998
In the oppressive heat of the Southeast United States, in a juvenile detention center called Camp Green Lake, a cruel warden makes her young prisoners dig holes throughout the desert. Unlucky offender Stanley Yelnats is accused of a theft he didn't commit, and his arrival at the camp really shakes things up for everyone.

Awards: Newbery Medal; National Book Award; *Bulletin of the Center for Children's Books*; Readers Choice Award for Teen Books (2002); *School Library Journal* Best Book of 1998; Voice of Youth Advocates Award.

Adaptations: *Holes* (film version), released 2003, Buena Vista Pictures

Stanley Yelnats' Survival Guide to Camp Green Lake: A Holes Companion Book, Bloomsbury, 2003

Small Steps, Delacorte Press, 2006

The Cardturner, Delacorte Press, 2010
Alton Richards, for lack of anything much better to do

one summer, is enlisted to help his wealthy uncle, Lester Trapp, as his "cardturner." Uncle Lester is a duplicate bridge player who has lost his sight due to diabetes. Along with the bond that grows between nephew and uncle, Alton also learns bridge and many life lessons along the way.

Awards: Alan Truscott Memorial Award (2010), presented by the International Bridge Press Association; 2011 American Library Association Best Fiction for Young Adults; Booklist Top 10 Sports Books for Youth, 2010; 2011 ALA Best Fiction for Young Adults; Children's Book Committee Bank Street College of Education Children's Choices, Best Books of 2011, Today, ages 12-14; Booklist 2010 Top 10 Books for Youth, Sports; *Publishers Weekly* Best Children's Books 2010, Fiction; *Publishers Weekly* Best Children's Books 2010

Fuzzy Mud, Delacorte Press, 2015

The Marvin Redpost Series

Kidnapped at Birth?, Random House, 1992

Why Pick on Me?, Random House, 1993

Is He a Girl?, Random House, 1993

Alone in His Teacher's House, Random House, 1994

Class President, Random House, 1999

A Flying Birthday Cake?, Random House, 1999

Super Fast Out of Control! Random House, 2000

A Magic Crystal?, Random House, 2000

The Wayside School Series

Sideways Stories from Wayside School, Wilcox & Follett, 1978
Thirty different chapters correspond to the setup of the unusual Wayside School, which is thirty stories high. The school was originally supposed to be thirty classrooms on one story, and that's only one of the school's unique features. Quirky students and teachers populate the pages of this first installment of the Wayside School series.

Wayside School Is Falling Down, Lothrop, Lee & Shepard, 1989
Awards: Arizona Young Readers' Chapter Book Award; Parents' Choice Award (1989)

Sideways Arithmetic from Wayside School,

Scholastic, 1989

More Sideways Arithmetic from Wayside School,
Scholastic, 1994

Wayside School Gets a Little Stranger, William
Morrow & Company, 1995
Students of Mrs. Jewls's class gets a successively
stranger series of substitute teachers when she
takes maternity leave. Meanwhile, the other
classes in Wayside School continue to experi-
ence the strange goings-on fans of the series
are used to and expect.
Awards: Buckeye Children's Book Award (Ohio);
Colorado Children's Book Award; Garden State
Children's Book Award (New Jersey); Golden
Archer Award (Wisconsin); Massachusetts
Children's Book Award; Young Hoosier Book
Award (Indiana)

Dogs Don't Tell Jokes

Dogs Don't Tell Jokes is an excellent choice for junior high readers, and Sachar's younger fans will enjoy it, too. —*School Library Journal*

There's a Boy in the Girls' Bathroom

In this humorous novel that tells of Bradley's learning to like himself and to make friends, Sachar ably captures both middle-grade angst and joy. The story is unusual, witty, and satisfying, if not always believable. —*School Library Journal*

Marvin Redpost: Alone in His Teacher's House

Readers will relate to the tension and reversal in the story. They'll recognize Marvin's feelings, both the humor of having to confront your teacher as a person and the sorrow at the death of a beloved pet. —*Booklist*

Fuzzy Mud

Clever petri dish design elements and multiplication equations sprinkled throughout the text help readers grasp the simple math that challenges science's claims of control. Featuring a plot that moves as fast as the ergonyms replicate, this issue-driven novel will captivate readers while giving them plenty to think about. —*School Library Journal*

Sachar expertly builds tension as he incrementally reveals the dangers of Biolene and its connection to fuzzy mud, ratcheting up the dangers facing Tamaya and her friends. Grounded in well-rounded central characters, this compelling novel holds as much suspense as fuel for discussion. —*Booklist*

Holes

Just when it seems as though this is going to be a weird YA cross between *One Flew Over the Cuckoo's Nest* and *Cool Hand Luke*, the story takes off—along with Stanley, who flees camp after his buddy Zero—in a wholly unexpected direction to become a dazzling blend of social commentary, tall tale and magic realism. —*Publishers Weekly*

A multitude of colorful characters coupled with the skillful braiding of ethnic folklore, American legend, and contemporary issues is a brilliant achievement. There is no question, kids will love *Holes*. —*School Library Journal*

1954 Louis Sachar is born in East Meadow, New York, to Robert and Ruth Raybin Sachar.

1963 The Sachar family moves to Tustin, Orange County, California.

1972 Robert Sachar dies; Louis returns home from Antioch College.

1973 Sachar begins school at the University of California at Berkeley.

1975 Sachar begins working at Hillside Elementary School as a teacher's aide.

1976 Sachar graduates from Berkeley with a B.A. in economics.

1976–1977 Sachar works at Beldoch Industries, in Norwalk, Connecticut.

1978 *Sideways Stories from Wayside School* is published; Sachar begins law school at Hastings College of Law in San Francisco.

1980 Sachar graduates from Hastings College of Law.

1981–1984 Sachar practices law part-time in San Francisco.

1985 Sachar marries Carla Askew.

1987 *There's a Boy in the Girls' Bathroom* is published by Alfred A. Knopf.
Their daughter, Sherre, is born.

1989 *The Boy Who Lost His Face* is published by Alfred A. Knopf.

1991 Sachar and his family move to Austin, Texas.

1995 Sachar begins work on *Holes*.

1998 *Holes* is published by Farrar, Straus and Giroux. Sachar wins the National Book Award.

1999 Sachar wins the Newbery Medal for *Holes*.

2001 Sachar begins work on the screenplay for *Holes*.

2003 The motion picture version of *Holes* comes out in April, to general acclaim.

2006 Sachar publishes *Small Steps*, a sequel to *Holes*.

2010 *The Cardturner* is published by Delacorte Press.

2015 Sachar releases his latest novel, *Fuzzy Mud*.

AMBIVALENT Having mixed feelings about something.

BRIDGE A popular card game played worldwide.

DEPOSITION Spoken testimony that is transcribed on paper and is used as evidence in a court case.

EMULATE To imitate

ESCALATE To increase by stages.

EXEMPLIFY To be an example of something.

FLIP Making light of something usually considered serious.

HINDERED Slowed down; delayed.

HORN BOOK MAGAZINE A critically acclaimed magazine established in 1924 that reviews and recommends the best new books published for children of all ages.

LAMENT To become sad or grieve about something.

LOOPY Silly, ridiculous, or absurd.

MAGIC REALISM Stories that combine realistic events with the fantastic or magical; sometimes also called magical realism.

MEAL TICKET A source of regular income.

NATIONAL BOOK AWARD The highest literary award that can be given to an American author.

NEWBERY MEDAL The highest award in American children's literature.

NUANCE Small details or shades of meaning that give depth to writing.

OPPRESSIVE Describes weather that is punishing and hard to deal with.

PALINDROME A word or phrase spelled the same forward and backward.

GLOSSARY

PREMISE Something upon which an argument is based or a conclusion that has been drawn.

PRESTIGIOUS Celebrated; important.

PUN A play on words that involves similar sense or sounds of words.

REPRIMAND A warning for doing something wrong.

RESILIENCE Toughness in the face of hardship.

SALVAGEABLE Able to be recovered or reused.

SAUNTERING Leisurely walking or strolling.

STIGMA A mark of shame or disgrace.

WRY Funny in an ironic way.

Canadian Library Association (CLA)
1150 Morrison Drive, Suite 400
Ottawa, ON K2H 8S9
(613) 232-9625
Website: http://www.cla.ca
The Canadian Library Assocation (CLA) champions
libraries via its efforts to influence public policy,
inspire and support member learning, and
foster collaboration among libraries throughout
Canada.

Canadian Society of Children's Authors, Illustrators
and Performers (CANSCAIP)
720 Bathurst Street, Suite 504
Toronto, ON M5S 2R4
Canada
(416) 515-1559
Website: http://www.canscaip.org
CANSCAIP supports children's literature in Canada,
including helping writers, via various media
efforts, both in print and online, as well as meet-
ings and conferences.

Farrar, Straus and Giroux
18 West 18th Street
New York, NY 10011
(212) 741-6900
Website: http://us.macmillan.com/fsg
Farrar, Straus and Giroux is an American publisher
whose sub-imprint Books for Young Readers
has released works by many popular

young-adult authors throughout the years, including Madeleine L'Engle, Roald Dahl, and Louis Sachar.

Penguin Random House
1745 Broadway
New York, NY 10019
(212) 782-9000
Website: http://www.penguinrandomhouse.com
Random House, now part of the merged Penguin Random House, has published many works by Louis Sachar through its Delacorte Press, Yearling, Random House Books for Young Readers, and Alfred A. Knopf imprints.

Society of Children's Book Writers and Illustrators (SCBWI)
8271 Beverly Boulevard
Los Angeles, CA 90048
(323) 782-1892
Website: http://www.scbwi.org
Society of Children's Book Writers and Illustrators is an international professional organization made up of authors and graphic artists creating primarily for young adults and children. It embraces practitioners in literature, magazines, film, and multimedia.

Young Adult Library Services Association (YALSA)/ American Library Association (ALA)
50 East Huron Street

Chicago, IL 60611
(800) 545-2433
Website: http://www.ala.org/yalsa
The Young Adult Library Services Association serves
to expand and support library services for
adolescent and teenage readers.

WEBSITES

Due to the changing nature of Internet links, the
Rosen Publishing Group, Inc., has developed an
online list of websites related to the subject of this
book. This site is updated regularly. Please use this
link to access the list:

http://www.rosenlinks.com/AAA/Sachar

Hagler, Gina. *Sarah Dessen* (All About the Author). New York, NY: Rosen Publishing, 2014.

Halverson, Deborah. *Writing Young Adult Fiction for Dummies*. Hoboken, NJ: For Dummies/Wiley Publishing, 2011.

Jordan, Denise M. *Walter Dean Meyers: A Biography of an Award-Winning Urban Fiction Author* (African-American Icons). New York, NY: Enslow Publishers, 2012.

La Bella, Laura. *Marissa Meyer* (All About the Author). New York, NY: Rosen Publishing, 2016.

Mead, Wendy. *Sharon Creech* (Spotlight on Children's Authors). New York, NY: Cavendish Square Publishing, 2014.

White, E. B. *Charlotte's Web*. New York, NY: HarperCollins, 2015.

Wolny, Philip. *James Dashner* (All About the Author). New York, NY: Rosen Publishing, 2014.

Wolny, Philip. *Stephen Chbosky* (All About the Author). New York, NY: Rosen Publishing, 2015.

"Biographical Essay: Louis Sachar." *Authors and Artists for Young Adults*, Volume 35. Farmington Hills, MI: Gale Group, 2000. Reproduced in Biography Resource Center. Retrieved July 2002 (http://galenet.galegroup. com).

Bolle, Sonja. "On the Set of 'Holes.'" *Publishers Weekly*, July 22, 2002, Vol. 249, No. 29, p. 81.

Children's Book Council. "Meet the Author: Louis Sachar." June 30, 2002. Retrieved July 2002 (http://www.cbcbooks.org/html/ louissachar .html).

Cooper, Ilene. "Review of *Sixth Grade Secrets*." *Booklist*, November 1, 1987, p. 484.

Cooper, Ilene. "Review of Someday Angeline." *Booklist*, September 1, 1983, p. 91.

Davis, Kate. "The *Holes* Story." *Read*, December 20, 2002, Vol. 52, No. 9, p. 12.

Dingus, Anne. "Louis Sachar." *Texas Monthly*, September 1999, Vol. 27, No. 19, p. 121.

Follos, Alison. "Review of *Holes*." *School Library Journal*, September 1998, p. 210.

Forman, Jack. "Review of *Johnny's in the Basement*." *School Library Journal*, December 1981, p. 68.

Gale, David. "Review of *There's a Boy in the Girls' Bathroom*." *School Library Journal*, April 1987, p. 103.

Hearne, Betsy. "He Didn't Do It." *New York Times*,

November 15, 1998, p. 52.

Hearne, Betsy. "Review of *There's a Boy in the Girls' Bathroom*." *Bulletin of the Center for Children's Books*, April 1987, p. 155.

Just, Julie. "An Interview with Louis Sachar." *New York Times*, January 15, 2006. Retrieved July 2015 (http://www.nytimes.com/2006/01/15/ books/review/sachar-interview.html?_r=0).

Kirkus Reviews. "Review of *There's a Boy in the Girls' Bathroom*." February 1, 1987, p. 224.

Kirkus Reviews. "Review of *Wayside School Gets a Little Stranger*." April 15, 1995, p. 562.

Kornfeld, Matilda, and Lillian Gerhardt. "Review of *Sideways Stories from Wayside School*." *School Library Journal*, September 1978.

Kowen, Kenneth E. "Review of *Marvin Redpost: Kidnapped at Birth?*" *School Library Journal*, March 1993, p. 186.

Martin, Claire. "Guide Handy for 'Holes' Frosh." *Denver Post*, April 27, 2003.

McElmeel, Sharon. "An Award Winning Author: Louis Sachar." *Book Report*, January/ February 2000, Vol. 8, No. 4, pp. 46–47.

Publishers Weekly. "Review of *Johnny's in the Basement*." August 12, 1983, p. 67.

Publishers Weekly. "Review of *Holes*." June 27, 1998, p. 78.

Publishers Weekly. "Review of *Sixth Grade Secrets*." August 28, 1987, p. 80.

Publishers Weekly. "Review of *Someday Angeline*."

August 12, 1983, p. 67.

Publishers Weekly. "The Cardturner." May 2010. Retrieved July 2015 (http://www.publishersweekly .com/978-0-385-73662-6).

Sachar, Louis. "Acceptance Speech." *Boston Globe–Horn Book Award.* Retrieved June 2002 (http:// www.hbook.com/ bghb_fiction.shtml).

Sachar, Louis. "Louis Sachar, Newbery Medal Acceptance." *Horn Book Magazine,* July 1999, Vol. 75, No. 4, p. 410.

Sachar, Sherre, and Carla Sachar. "Louis Sachar." *Horn Book Magazine,* July/August 1999, Vol. 75, No. 4, pp. 418–422.

Scholastic Teachers. "Louis Sachar's Interview Transcript." Retrieved July 15, 2002 (http:// www.scholastic.com).

Stevenson, Deborah. "Review of *Marvin Redpost: Why Pick on Me?*" *Bulletin of the Center for Children's Books,* February 1993, pp. 167–168.

Stevenson, Deborah. "Review of *Wayside School Gets a Little Stranger.*" *Bulletin of the Center for Children's Books,* March 1995, p. 248.

Strickland, Barbara. "Louis Sachar: Top of His Class." *Austin Chronicle,* February 26, 1999. Retrieved June 10, 2015 (http://www.austin-chronicle.com/books/1999-02-26/521429).

Sutton, Roger. "Review of *Holes.*" *Bulletin of the Center for Children's Books,* September/ October, 1998, pp. 593–595.

U.S. News & World Report. "Louis Sachar." February

15, 1999, Vol. 126, No. 6, p. 12.

U*X*L Junior DISCovering Authors.U*X*L "Louis Sachar." 1998. Reproduced in Discovering Collection. Farmington Hills, MI: Gale Group. December 2000. Retrieved July 2002 (http://galenet.galegroup.com).

Writing. "Paint a Picture for the Reader: A Conversation with Louis Sachar." November/December 2002 Teacher's Guide, Vol. 25, No. 3, p. 26.

ABOUT THE AUTHORS

Philip Wolny is a writer and editor from Queens, New York City. His other author biography for Rosen Publishing is *Stephen Chbosky*.

Meg Greene is an author living in Virginia.

PHOTO CREDITS

Designer: Nicole Russo; Editor: Philip Wolny; Photo Researcher: Philip Wolny